Life 101 Affirmations

Life Improvements

Marriage Matters

Parenting

Spiritual Growth

Healing/Relaxation

By Bonnie L. Bair

Life Improvements

Galesburg, Illinois

Names: Bair, Bonnie L. | Bair, Bonnie L. editor

Title: Life 101 Affirmations | by Bonnie L. Bair, LCPC

Description: 2nd edition. | Galesburg; Illinois: Life Improvements, 2017

Identifiers: LCCN 2017917942 print |5 compact discs | e(book)

IBSN 978-0-999-4772-2-9

Dedicated to Todd & Amanda

Life 101 Affirmations

Special Thanks to God.

Chapter 1   Life Improvements

These affirmations are designed to provide a vision for establishing and reinforcing behaviors that support happy and healthy relationships and lives. As you review these affirmations on a regular basis, the quicker and easier behavior change becomes. Expect your life to wonderfully Improve!

Bonnie L. Bair, LCPC

I respect and affirm myself. I practice positive self-talk, think about my successes and competently face challenges. I trust my own intuition.

I am glad to be who I am. I enjoy being with myself.

I am willing to grow. I am refreshed and healthy. I rest, as needed. I eat lightly and exercise regularly.

I prepare and I'm on schedule. I take time for thanksgiving and communicate my trust in God.

I let go of fear and anxiety (by breathing, saying a prayer, emptying my mind and by doing something).

I manage stress by assessing my thoughts and creating thoughts that lead to a calmer, more relaxed, life.

I talk about my feelings, work off anger, exercise, and take time for relaxation and play.

I create positive expectations for health and healing. I open myself to humor, friendship, and love.

I think and speak positively. I'm understanding and compassionate.

I assume the best about and speak well of others.

I listen to others fully without judging. I accept each person as he or she is. I reduce distractions, if possible. I listen for ideas, concepts and feelings. I reflect the information shared by the speaker and ask for clarification if needed. I accept responsibility for myself and not others.

If a person is angry, I respond with gentleness and understanding. I give them permission to feel angry. Anger is energy from fear or hurt. It is a flag that something is not right.

I may express understanding by being surprised the person doesn't feel worse. (This makes it okay to be upset). I then request more information. Allowing the person to talk, often diffuses the anger so that more conversation can take place. I remember, anger is a normal emotion.

When I find myself getting angry, I breathe deeply and completely.

If I'm angry with another person, I tell them how I am feeling. I am specific about what might be causing the feeling - without blaming the other person. I may say something like, "I may have misinterpreted what you were saying."

I respectfully assert myself in conflict. I handle verbal putdowns by telling the person I don't understand and ask what they mean by the statement. I agree with the true portions of a critique. I choose my words wisely. I am responsible for my side of the relationship.

I take a break, when I need it, by telling the other person I need to collect my thoughts for a moment and will return in 5 minutes to finish our conversation. While breaking, I let my body go and practice getting limp all over. This helps me calm down. I then assume a need to learn more. I ask myself what the other person cares about.

Upon returning, I ask about/or acknowledge the other person's needs. I express myself in an honest straightforward manner, without exaggeration. I use "I statements," to express what I feel, think, want, and need. This decreases the chance of being misunderstood.

I acknowledge behavior or situations that contribute to difficulty, without blaming anyone for the situation or conflict. I tell the other person what I desire and why. When I'm the responsible party for the problem, I say "I'm sorry and here is what I am going to do differently in the future." Being responsible and consistent, over time, will increase the trust between us.

We may put information down on paper, to better assess the things we each face, or to create an action plan to address various issues. We can write down acceptable solutions.

I can also dissolve anger by separating myself from the irritating source, working, exercising, or talking to someone I trust.

I reduce anxiety by taking deep breaths, acknowledging and feeling my feelings, telling myself the truth, and taking responsibility for my own actions. I let go of others and allow them to be who they are.

I acknowledge and examine the thoughts that accompany my feelings and figure out what I need to do.

I make any changes within myself, that are necessary, and I ask others if I need something from them.

I'm responsible for my life and my choices. I address concerns as soon as possible, and make changes as needed. I allow myself to take risks and I am confident in my decision-making abilities.

I resolve or let go of hurts from the past. I forgive offenses and allow myself to grieve and accept reality. I release burdens and cares. I give myself permission to move into the new and enjoy life.

When feeling frustrated or stressed, I stop and breathe completely and deeply.

I discipline myself to rest and I practice relaxing. I willingly let go of negative habit patterns and learn new healthy habits.

I find peace within myself and I approve of myself, unconditionally. I smile and maintain a state of peace, so I can perform at my best. I have feelings of well-being and a balanced fulfilling life. I expect things to go well, and they do.

I slow down, keep things in perspective and make life easier. I take responsibility for myself and allow others to do the same. I ask for help when I need it.

I live in harmony with those around me. I give and receive love.

I honor others by listening to them, paraphrasing their words and responding with something positive. This conveys and attitude of respect.

I think first and then respond. I speak with clarity, grace, and confidence. I pay attention and show interest in, and am compassionate to others.

I serve others when I can do so with a smile.

I'm understanding of others by accepting their limitations and by being sensitive to their needs. I'm fair toward those whose opinions and beliefs differ from mine. I go the extra mile and respond to unkindness with love. I avoid blaming. I accept and acknowledge my own feelings. I'm kind to myself and seek and attract mutually satisfying relationships with family and friends.

I am gentle and understanding with myself. I respect myself by managing my time and priorities effectively and easily. I understand this may occasionally require me to say, "No," gracefully or to reschedule at times. I communicate honestly and clearly. I work through disagreement constructively.

I inspire teamwork and am flexible. I surround myself with positive influences and choose win/win situations and solutions with others.

My habits serve me well. I do what I enjoy.

I listen to my conscience and follow my instincts.

I set reasonable expectations for myself. I pray about and write out my plans, goals, and dreams (specifically and clearly).

I deliberately chose to think positively and visualize my dreams as being met.

I eliminate clutter and I follow through with my goals. I divide difficult tasks into small segments and complete them with ease.

I deliberately make my life light, easy, and joyful. I think of the things I am thankful for.

I make decisions that support my values and health. I lovingly care for my physical, emotional, and spiritual needs. I think on what is true, lovely, and praise worthy. I eat nutritiously and sleep peacefully. I wake up feeling refreshed and energized.

I practice breathing fully. This helps me think clearly, relax, and make wise decisions. I ask for what I want and need. I seek assistance as necessary.

I think about my life and self with confidence and joy. I am happy, healthy, and prosperous. As I renew my mind, my life changes for the better. I confidently expect problems to be solved, obstacles removed, and goals achieved.

As I nourish myself, others are nourished. I share my life with others and they are blessed. I'm inspired to say and do the right thing at the right time.

I work to make my life better, and it is. I believe all things are possible.

I take myself to a quiet place each day to connect with God.

I go for walks and enjoy nature.

I allow myself to know, enjoy, and fulfill God's purpose for my life.

I read God's word and feel God's presence in my life.

I admit difficulties to God. I pray about every concern with thanksgiving and then I purposely think about something else. I allow God to strengthen, soothe, encourage, teach, and refresh me.

I value and enjoy my life and work. I love what I do.

My mind is clear and body relaxed. I practice deep and complete breathing. I exercise, sing, laugh, and play.

My life is simple and ordered (with variety). I maintain mental creativity and emotional flexibility, through good nutrition, exercise, and mental stimulation.

I care about the environment by recycling and using resources wisely.

I create fun in my life and relationships. I look for ways to show love, kindness, and affection. I communicate clearly and lovingly, with family and friends.

If someone asks personal questions of me I prefer not to answer, I remain call and stay quiet or gracefully change the subject.

If someone rejects me (my thoughts, or choices), I maintain my self-esteem.

I reduce negative emotions by thinking positive, remaining objective, and thinking of my blessings.

I see temporary setbacks as a sign to try something else or go in another direction. I ask myself what I can do to ensure success.

I omit the word "should" from my vocabulary, and let go of complaining. I'm responsible for my own actions. I choose how I want to act, think, feel and behave. I make decisions that are in my best interest.

When interrupted, I remain calm, breathe, and prioritize. I may ask the person if they can wait until I finish what I'm doing and give them an idea of how long it will take. Or I schedule a different time to address their concern.

When 2-3 people want something from me and I'm trying to complete a task and the phone rings, I take a deep breath and prioritize. I remain calm, and make wise decisions confidently. I ask for help when I need it.

I learn to have fun and manage interruptions with grace and ease.

I let others take care of their own responsibilities and feel their own feelings.

If someone tries to make me feel guilty or manipulate me, I can calmly ask, you're not trying to make me feel guilty, are you? Or, you're not trying to manipulate me, are you? This will help the other person become aware of how they are interacting with me and will help establish healthier ways of communicating.

When I need time to think or prepare before I respond to another, I tell the other person I will need to think about it or check on something. I schedule a later time to meet with the person.

I teach others the morality of self-acceptance by setting an example of it in myself. I respect myself and others respect me.

I make a habit out of enjoying life and being good to myself.

When someone compliments me, I think about the compliment, smile, and say, "thank you!"

If someone has a bad day, I do what I can and say a prayer for him or her.

When someone gets off key, I strive to stay on key and do my part. People are responsible for their own behavior and their own lives.

I reduce frustration, by remembering I have choices. I remember the limitations of human beings. I address concerns immediately, adjust my behavior, ask for what I want, and stand up for issues that are important to me.

When disappointed with my actions, I apologize by asking for forgiveness, and amending my ways.

I quickly forgive myself, implement change and move forward.

When facing a big or small decision, I get peaceful first and then decide. I remember frustration may be part of the problem-solving process. I ask God to help me think, when overwhelmed, and ask for right thoughts, words, and actions.

I neutralize negative emotions by substituting with positive thoughts, prayer, listening to affirmations, assessing causes, and remaining objective. I make a goal list, take purposeful action, and one day at a time.

I stop worry and obsession. I am proactive. I identify the source of irritations and address problems immediately. I feed my mind information needed to make decisions. I feed my mind healthy thoughts, and learn new things.

I reduce fear and worry by moving confidently in the direction of my dreams. I breathe deeply and say I can do this. I move in the direction that feels right and willingly face challenges objectively and earnestly.

I am decisive and decide what I want and I create habits that will help me achieve my goals.

I think well and figure things out. I figure out what I need to do and when to do it. I write my goals down, in small steps, with completion dates.

I perform according to my hopes. I affirm positively, visualize clearly, and breathe deeply.

I have enough talent, intelligence and resources to fulfill my destiny. I am enough and have enough. I am free to be who I am. I stand tall with confidence and am courageous and competent.

I learn from mistakes and correct my own thinking and behavior. I am open to learning from others.

I care for myself and keep in mind what my responsibilities are. I realize the more I give purposeful direction to my subconscious mind through affirmations, the faster I will see those things happen in my life.

I say what it is that I want to know. For instance, if I want to know how to do something, I say I know how to do whatever it is. My subconscious mind then helps me figure it out and I know how to, or learn how to, perform the task quicker.

I have what it takes to do what I desire, and do it well. I use my time well. Goals give me direction and purpose.

I remember that less is more. I reduce clutter, simplify my life, and spend only that which I can afford. I use what I learn to adjust, adapt, and grow.

To keep from being pushed to the wire, I keep urgent things to a minimum. I diligently care for the non-urgent, but important things.

I schedule fun in my life, concentrate on the can-do portions of tasks, and remember there is time to do the things I need and want to do.

I trust and listen to myself and to my needs.

I look for people who can help me. I choose those who are capable to do the job and who can work in a spirit of truth and harmony.

I create opportunities to make life brighter, smoother, and more enjoyable for those around me. I am thoughtful and dependable. My giving is beneficial.

I make wise choices and think sensibly. My eyes are good and my mind sound. I have a spirit of power and love.

I accept God's unconditional love. God is continually watching everything that concerns me and has everlasting love for me.

I pray for God's guidance, am calm and confident. I have a clear sense of direction and handle any situation that comes my way. I enjoy learning.

I exercise my mind, body, and spirit.

I prosper and am in good health. I eat nuts, fruits, vegetables and grains. I remember to drink plenty of water.

I read God's word and get sunshine and fresh air.

I enjoy each, and every day.

Life Improvements Resources

Assertiveness Skills: Nelda Shelton, Sharon Burton

Bi-Monthly Publication; Kate McVeigh Ministries

Boosting Your Listening Power; Correspondent, July/August 1998

Co-dependent No More; Melody Beattie

Eleven Ways to Ease Your Nerves & Mind; National Association for Mental Health

Getting Together, Building Relationships that Get to Yes; Fisher & Brown

Holy Bible; God's Word written in various translations

How to Do What You Want to Do, & Standing Up for Yourself; Dr. Paul Hauck

Overcoming Anger & Frustration; Dr. Paul Hauck

The Psychology of Achievement; Brian Tracy, MA

Twenty-One Ways to Diffuse Anger and Calm People Down; Career Track

You Can Heal Your Life; Louise Hay

Winning Without Intimidation; Bob Burg

Notes

Chapter 2 Marriage Matters

Challenges come when two people try to live together. These affirmations are designed to provide a vision for establishing and reinforcing behaviors that support happy/healthy relationships and lives. As you review these affirmations on a regular basis, the quicker and easier behavior change becomes. Expect your life to wonderfully improve!

Bonnie L. Bair, LCPC

Our Marriage is a partnership. We are committed and faithful to each other.

We make decisions that support our relationship.

We work together to utilize each other's strengths and talents.

We acknowledge and appreciate each other's efforts and challenges.

We speak well of each other, and ourselves.

We talk to each other in courteous ways and treat each other with gentleness, patience and compassion.

We express and address concerns right away, to maintain optimal health and happiness in our relationship.

We say a prayer before we raise and important issue.

We breathe deeply to help stay calm and think clearly.

We use ally signals to say something's not right, and let's talk; or to say, I need a time out to think.

We clear the air by focusing on the issues, talking things through, and assuming the best of each other.

We listen carefully and communicate without blaming or manipulating.

We use examples and stories to communicate our thoughts and feelings, clearly.

We listen until there is new understanding and communicate to the other what our new understanding is.

We realize that because people are different, it's okay to disagree at times. We can agree to disagree. Whenever possible, we negotiate a solution.

We may write down the pros and cons of an issue to help stay focused and reach an agreement.

We accept feelings as normal and sometimes transient. By accepting and acknowledging our own feelings, we deal with emotions more effectively.

Talking about our emotions clearly and honestly, helps us ensure success with future interactions.

We keep in mind what we know to be true and we listen to each other carefully, without interruptions.

We ask questions such as: what, when, how, where, etc. We tell our spouse what they say, feel, and need, in our own words. This makes sure we understand each other correctly.

We take turns and both say what we think, feel, and need with ease.

We speak truthfully with each other, are clear and direct.

We use "I statements" like, "I think, I feel, or I need." We ask each other for what we want, tell each other what it will mean to us, and tell each other how we will feel when we get it.

We accept responsibility for behaviors that have contributed to difficulty and remember to ask for forgiveness.

We forgive each other and we adjust our own behaviors.

We write down our ideas, so we can remember and make changes as needed.

We brainstorm and find win/win solutions together.

We value each other's unique abilities and viewpoints.

We think and talk about the things that make us feel good about ourselves and about what we are grateful for.

We affirm each other in the way the other needs affirmed (with a smile, touch, gift, compliment, thank you, hug, etc.).

We make a habit of thinking positively about each other, our relationship, and ourselves. We actively choose to improve our lives.

I take care of my health, so I'm at my best for my spouse.

I feed my mind, body, and spirit with good things.

I eat nutritiously, supplement my diet as necessary, and drink plenty of water.

I get adequate rest, exercise, and time in nature.

My choice of exercise reduces stress and improves the quality of our lives.

I connect with God daily. We learn, practice, and share spiritual truths with each other.

We make time for each other. We do not overextend ourselves. We manage our time well, by meeting our needs and priorities. We allow ourselves to say, "No," to others, and we schedule time for quiet and rest.

We allow ourselves to hire help, as needed.

We respect each other for the way each meets their responsibilities.

We admire and praise each other for who they are, what they've accomplished, and what they mean to us.

We discover each other's desires, talk often of our dreams, and work together to make them happen.

We write down specific goals with achievement dates.

We enjoy reaching our personal and mutual goals.

We value each other's time and are considerate of each other's priorities.

We allow each other to be an individual and make sure the other has time to do the things they enjoy.

We enjoy our time alone and together. We develop and maintain friendships with people who are supportive of our relationship.

We shut the door on negative thinking. We practice relaxation techniques, such as; quiet time, listening to affirmations, and visualizing our goals as met.

We react to various situations with positive action.

We both work to eliminate clutter, pay off debts, and keep our living space clean. We help each other make unpleasant tasks more enjoyable.

We have frequent honest communication regarding money, goals, etc. We agree on guidelines for spending, giving, saving, and investing.

We put our money to work for us, so it grows. We buy only what we can afford. We take advantage of opportunities, live below our means, save, and invest wisely.

We talk to each other about difficulties and provide each other with support and involvement.

We expose ourselves to positive influences and seek outside expertise as necessary.

We ask each other for help when we need it.

We look for ways to make our lives and marriage better. We act on ideas as they come to us.

We often sense what the other is thinking and feeling.

We ask about and notice the things the other values (gifts, quality time together, words of encouragement, acts of service, or physical attention).

We then communicate and demonstrate our love for them in ways they most like and desire. This helps them feel loved and appreciated.

We cooperate and take turns planning and participating in activities the other enjoys.

We ask each other what we can do to make our relationship more enjoyable.

We remember to compliment and thank each other often.

In response we smile and say, "Thank you!" or "You're Welcome!"

We remember to look in each other's eyes and greet each other with a smile.

We tell each other things like "I love you! I believe in you!"

We do things for each other, spend time alone together, and give gifts to each other. We give attention, words of affection, and understanding to each other

I affirm my spouse in the ways they most need and desire.

We accept and respond to each other with love.

I am romantic with my wife. I do special things to show my love to her.

I provide my wife with emotional support, conversation, and admiration. I build her ego and help her feel like a lady. I take her out to dinner, make sure she gets recreation, and tell her I love and appreciate her.

I admire and praise my husband.

I provide my husband with deep respect and honor. I build his ego and help him feel like the man he is. I listen to him, accept his decisions, express appreciation for the things he does, and give him physical attention.

We tell each other about our needs. We lovingly treat each other's needs, feelings, and concerns as one with our own.

Our actions reflect love and admiration.

We acknowledge each other's efforts and accomplishments.

We remember to tell each other what we specifically like about the person they are, and what we like that they do.

We work to build trust and seek to meet each other's deepest spiritual, emotional, and physical needs.

We initiate sexual advances with looks of love, tenderness, and with verbal connection.

We enjoy each other and our time together. We hold hands, say kind words, comfort, and encourage each other. We share touches, smiles, massages, hugs, and kisses.

We trust each other and our needs are met.

We pray, laugh, and play together.

We do what we love, and our lives are balanced and fulfilling.

Marriage Matters Resources

Assertiveness Skills: Nelda Shelton, Sharon Burton

Boosting Your Listening Power; Correspondent, July/August 1998

Co-dependent No More; Melody Beattie

Getting Together, Building Relationships that Get to Yes; Fisher & Brown

Holy Bible; God's Word written in various translations

Honeymoon Marriage; Darrin and Donna McNeese

Standing Up for Yourself; Dr. Paul Hauck

Overcoming Anger & Frustration; Dr. Paul Hauck

Straight Talk to Men and Their Wives; Dr. James Dobson

The Five Love Languages; Gary Chapman

The Power of We; David J. Ludwig

Chapter 3 Parenting

Affirmations assist individuals with behavior change or reinforcement. These affirmations are designed by a Licensed Counselor to help you become a more effective parent. As you listen to these affirmations regularly, your parenting success will increase and you will more fully enjoy being a parent.

Bonnie L. Bair, LCPC

Teaching Values/Being Healthy

I celebrate my child as a gift and I value my child's personality.

I have an attitude of respect toward my child and wonder toward their world.

I use playfulness in my parenting, to teach values and encourage cooperation.

I give my child limits, guidance, and structure. I apply these in a loving and relaxed way.

I keep the lines of communication open with my child.

I encourage them to talk about their thoughts and feelings, and to speak up about their needs.

I'm available when my child wants to talk.

I stop talking and take time to sit and listen.

I provide my child with loving eye contact and focused uninterrupted attention.

I ask my child questions that require a response different from yes or no.

I let my child finish their thoughts without interrupting.

I generously give my child love and affection.

I physically touch my child to communicate my love. Snuggling, foot & back rubs can do wonders.

I give hugs and kisses or wrestle with and tickle my child.

Showing affection and attention to my child is vital to their well-being.

This helps my child learn independence and self-dependence.

I'm a reasonable person and parent.

I communicate clearly and share feelings with my child. I share my agenda with my child.

I honor my child's, as well as my own boundaries and limits. This models healthy relationships.

When something's not working right, we sit down together and figure out a workable solution for the both of us.

I use empathy with my child, by acknowledging their feelings.

I listen and pause before replying and asking questions.

I paraphrase what my child has said in my own words, to my child.

I establish reasonable limits; lovingly and respectfully.

I give my child simple/clear expectations.

I am calm and consistent. I set limits without guilt and realize that protests are inevitable.

(Non-compliance is an important part of a child's development. It helps children build assertiveness and acquire social skills to help them face bullies.)

I tell my child (clearly) what I expect and I follow through with my decisions.

I praise behavior immediately, consistently, and specifically.

I model the behavior I want to teach and I reward behavior I like.

I teach my child to obey.

I teach my child that God sees and hears everything and know their thoughts.

I encourage and inspire confidence in my child by teaching my child responsibility.

I encourage my child to accept tough challenges by emphasizing that trying is the goal.

I praise my child for working hard on a problem rather than being smart or good at something. This will help my child view difficulties as surmountable and not the result of some skill or talent he/she lacks.

I allow my child to make decisions and encourage my child to contribute to the family.

I help my child organize their things and provide a quiet space for my child to study or think.

I remember to talk with other parents for ideas and support.

I set a good example.

I feel good about and take care of myself.

I learn from and forgive my own mistakes. I share these with my child.

I demonstrate empathy for others and treat others with patience and respect.

I surround myself with positive influences and enjoy and value my work.

I accept, appreciate, and cherish my child.

I protect my child from unhealthy influences and give my child what they need. This prevents future difficulties.

I purposely slow down to enjoy my child and the other pleasures in life.

Discipline

Effective discipline interrupts behavior patterns and leads to conversation and connection.

Children who feel connected also feel inclined to be cooperative and thoughtful.

My child or myself, can call a meeting on the couch at any time (as a mutual timeout or prevention strategy).

When I call a meeting, I present the difficulty to my child as a joint problem requiring a solution.

This helps things go smoother.

I make eye contact, talk softly, and hold my child as gently as possible.

I focus on and find the underlying need or feeling underneath my child's behavior.

We, then, can both focus on the outcomes we hope to achieve.

This meeting helps build connection with each other and empowers my child.

I remember, the essence of discipline is to teach.

I set fair consistent limits and give adequate explanations of such.

Whenever possible, I deliver discipline prior to getting upset and do so clearly, calmly and briefly.

If I'm upset, I take a 20 second break, breathe, think, and pray.

I refrain from arguing over rules. I focus on getting my child's attention.

I am consistent and fair. I acknowledge my child's needs.

I don't humiliate or malign my child. Instead I focus on behavior and state things matter-of-factly.

I praise in public and correct in private, whenever possible.

The discipline I choose, enhances my relationship with my child.

I avoid arguing and speak to my child when we are both calm.

Whenever possible, I keep a playful rather than harsh tone with my child. This maintains connection.

For example: I wonder what made a fine boy like you forget what he was supposed to do.

I stay connected with my child, while setting limits.

I help my child evaluate consequences and accept responsibility.

Rather than regularly threatening my child, I am specific about directions and I state how my child and I will feel when a task is completed.

I make simple observations and non-judgmental statements about bedtime and cleaning-up. Instead of saying the room is a mess, I say there are toys on the floor.

I compliment my child on specific things I see them doing. I give descriptive compliments frequently.

When I do give a warning, I follow through with it.

I give my child a clean slate once consequences are over.

Dealing with Emotions

I teach my child how to deal with emotions by sharing how I am feeling with my child and by accepting responsibility for my own feelings and actions.

When disappointments or failures happen, I see them as stepping-stones and look for the benefit or lesson in them and teach my child to do the same.

I encourage my child to talk about their full range of emotions, anger, disappointment, frustration, or tiredness.

When my child is really upset; I label intense feelings without judging them, like: I can see you're really, mad now.

I accept my child's strong feelings and let them flow.

I remind my child that crying, being afraid, and being angry are all-okay.

I hold my child gently and firmly if aggressive toward someone.

I think helpful thoughts. I remember that although I don't like something, I can stand anything. This helps me cope with stressful situations and helps me make good decisions.

When I find myself thinking negatively, I stop and take a deep breath. I acknowledge my feelings, take another deep breath, and think of how I can handle the situation for a positive outcome.

When my small child exhibits frustration, I sit close, breathe, and remain calm. I let my child vent. This helps my child heal, release emotions, and dissolve tension. This is not behavior to be punished. I ask my child what they are feeling. This allows my child to act out emotions. I provide my child with more workable ways to handle feelings (like banging on a drum or pillow.)

Since children may stop throwing tantrums when they feel as if they really have been heard, I let tantrums run their natural course to completion.

I stay with my child, am calm, quiet and gentle. I get my child something to eat if I think they are hungry.

I stay calm while being firm and emotionally available to my child.

This teaches my child they will not be left alone in their dark night of the soul.

I encourage my child that nothing inside them is too awful to share with me – not even overwhelming feelings of frustration.

I do not take angry words or aggression personally. Since, aggression is often taken out on the people closest to them.

When my child exhibits unwanted behavior, I use the most minimal intervention I can.

I remain calm and breathe.

I ask: if that knot in your throat could talk what would it say. If the butterflies in your stomach did a dance, what would it look like?

I make use of quiet time to breathe and help calm my child or myself.

I play with my child to help my child work through feelings or aggression.

Once my child has calmed down, I teach alternative behaviors that I want my child to do, through positive feedback and direct instruction.

I teach my child to put words to their feelings and teach how to cope with anger in healthy ways such as drawing a picture, running, playing the drums, breathing, removing self from irritating situation, etc.

If I am emotionally charged, I put off conversation until we both are calm. A pause can be life-saving and keeps me on my feet and my feet out of my mouth.

Waiting allows me to evaluate my choices and make better decisions.

I know when to keep quiet. The words I say help others.

I also use words that encourage growth, such as: How do you plan on handling that? Or how do you think that will work?

I avoid arguing and I speak to my child when we are both calm.

Interactions with Others

I tolerate a certain amount of grumbling. As, long as, it is not disrespectful.

Whining happens when kids can't quite get out the feelings and can't be happy either.

I encourage my child to state what they want in a more pleasing way.

I encourage talk about emotions and using a strong cheerful voice to get what they want.

I acknowledge my child's feelings.

I teach my child how to deal with anger. I teach them to verbalize what they are unhappy about, work off the tension in a positive way, and adopt helpful thoughts.

When frustrated, I stop and breathe. This helps me think clearly. I ask for help if I need it. I take a time out and return to approach the challenge differently.

I teach my child to breathe completely when feeling stressed (like when blowing bubbles).

I encourage my child to use breathing exercises.

I reward my child for practicing breathing exercises.

I point out to my child when I handle anger or frustration effectively myself. This models appropriate behavior.

I take time to pretend being angry, by asking for something in a calm and pleasant voice.

I teach my child to protect their self with calm yet firm words.

I teach my child alternative ways of getting what they want; like how to get my attention when I'm talking to someone else, etc.

I strategically plan with my child how to handle different circumstances or events.

I remind my child of their right to feel safe at school and encourage them to solve their problems.

I teach them how to use humor and how to walk away during certain situations

I encourage my child to speak up for their self and keep body limits.

I remind my child to pay attention to their feelings and only do the things my child feels good about doing.

I offer my small child solutions, when playing with others, and challenge my child to find solutions for themselves that are good for everyone.

I am clear about how I feel with my child. This teaches my child how to be clear about how they feel and what they need from others. This helps them convey how they want to be treated. This also helps my child be effective and able to solve their own problems - not afraid of conflict and strong emotions, and not afraid of the big bad bully.

I teach my child not to give up their possessions too readily.   For example, I have my child practice saying I'm using this right now, etc.

If my child complains about being called a name. I ask my child if they believe it.

If my child complains that someone hit them, I ask if they are hurt?

I teach my child that what they think determines how they feel, not what others say about them.

I teach my child emotional skills, playing skills, and basic safety.

I teach them to let younger siblings or friends be, "in charge" of play, sometimes.

I intervene between siblings, or others, when overpowering is taking place. Without taking sides, I respond with things like this behavior is not okay. Everyone needs a turn or everyone needs to play safe.

I teach, our "house rules" say, "Treat Everyone with Respect!"

I teach my child how to take turns, share, follow directions, and win and lose gracefully.

I allow myself to be silly and play with my child. Play helps children learn and understand emotions and the world.

I give my child space and time to think and express feelings.

I protect, approve of, and listen to my child.

I listen to my intuition, am guided by love, and love my child - no matter what.

When I'm feeling upset, and I do not understand the reason for something, I may choose to look at things from a different perspective.

I acknowledge feelings and I replace negative and depressing thoughts with positive promises from God's word. I teach my child to do likewise.

Family Time

I provide a safe fun place for my child to play.

I give my child opportunities to be in charge, to help maintain closeness and confidence.

I make sure my family has down time for emotionally enriching experiences.

I read with my child, watch TV with my child, and take time to play games etc. with my child.

I safeguard what my child watches and hears.

I provide my child with healthy activities, to keep their interest and prevent difficulties.

I practice listening to my child and regularly stop what I am doing to listen to my child.

I acknowledge my child's words and feelings, by telling them what I understood them to say or feel.

I keep from giving much advice, to give them opportunities to problem solve.

I enjoy spending time with my child. And I let my child know I enjoyed talking, playing or being with them.

Our communication reflects our trust in each other and God.

I make sure my child feels, and is regarded as, important to the family.

I provide my child with healthy nutrition and positive influences. I make sure my child gets proper rest.

I teach my child to eat nutritiously and provide my child with proteins and complex carbohydrates, such as fresh or frozen fruits and vegetables, and breads made with unbleached flour. I encourage my child to drink plenty of water.

I make every effort to have the family eat together and have each person take a part in the preparation or cleanup of a meal.

I have my child prepare for bedtime one hour prior to going to sleep. Before my child goes to sleep, I ask my child to talk about the best part of the day and to think of the things they did that made them feel proud.

I teach my child to love doing the right things and to be responsible.

I teach my child how to make decisions, manage their time, solve problems, organize themselves, be healthy, communicate clearly, and set and respect boundaries.

I give my child choices and teach that we share, tell the truth, keep our promises, and meet our responsibilities.

I teach how to gather knowledge, prepare, persist and achieve. I encourage my child to learn to succeed through personal thinking and learning.

I teach my child God's word and pray for my child.

I love my child for who they are, not for how they perform. I build on my child's strengths.

I show my child they are special by my words and actions.

I am patient, negotiate with, and correct my child, in a lovingly manner.

I express belief in their abilities and encourage their dreams.

I value my child's opinions, and encourage them to share thoughts and feelings.

I give feed back to my child, about what they said. In return, I have them tell me what they learned.

I make learning interesting and fun.

I'm a good parent. My actions are purposeful.

I share my goals, plans, and successes with my child.

I have the courage and ability to make changes for the betterment of my family and myself.

I ignore setbacks. I use them as stepping-stones, and concentrate my efforts in positive ways.

I teach my child about delayed gratification and teach them problem solving strategies like: identifying the problem or challenge, thinking of the possibilities, and identifying choices. I teach how to plan for things and evaluate outcomes

I'm a creative problem solver and find win/win solutions.

When frustrated, I stop and breathe. This helps me to think clearly. I ask for help if I need it. I take a time out and calmly return to approach the challenge differently.

When feeling overwhelmed, I make a list and prioritize.

I do my best and what I can. I pray about and let go of the rest.

I slow down and remember to enjoy the roses and small pleasures along the way.

I maintain my sense of humor and make a habit of smiling.

I praise and encourage my child for the positive things they do. I encourage them to keep trying in the areas that are difficult.

I encourage my child that they are going to do good work and accomplish great things by saying things like: "You can do it," or "I believe in you."

I nurture my child's creativity.

I teach them to view the world's problems as motivation for problem solving.

Whenever there is a problem with my child, I look inside myself to see if there is something in me that could be causing the situation.

I spend time talking, and listening to my child. This prevents much trouble.

This is my core job. I listen patiently as I have all the time in the world. I ask questions like, "What are you going to do? Is there something I can help you with? How do you mean? How do you feel?" etc. This increases bonding and increases my child's self-esteem.

While loving my child with a continual flow of love and acceptance, I set clear limits of expected behavior.

I reward good behavior, in a way my child values.

I reach out to others for advice, when I need it.

I teach my child the importance of exercising, by exercising with my child. Exercise increases pleasantness and feelings of well-being. Exercise increases energy and helps us to sleep better and interact more harmoniously.

I schedule personal playtime for family members, and myself, in which everyone does something on their own.

I teach my child to like their self and treat themselves with patience and understanding.

I admit when I'm wrong and apologize for what I have said or done that hurt them or made them feel bad about themselves in anyway. This increases my child's love and respect for me.

I ask my child what I can do to be a better parent, and I ask if I do anything they don't like. This gives them the opportunity to express feeling and myself the opportunity to re-evaluate my ways.

I ask myself what I can do, to be a better parent.

I consciously choose and practice being the best parent I can be.

I help my child reach their full potential by making sure my child feels safe at home and school.

I protect my child from the adult world.

I make sure my child's education and entertainment is uplifting and fun.

I create an environment in which my child feels they belong.

I set positive outcomes and set clear, reasonable values and boundaries.

I help my child develop spiritually.

I build routine into our lives.

I do what is important.

Parenting is Fun. I take time to laugh. It helps me stay healthy and creative.

I accept and cherish my child, how they are. I show them continual love.

I carefully listen and am affectionate with them.

I spend time with each child individually.

I seek to understand my child.

I expect good things of my child.

I show and tell my child I love them.

I practice optimism and smiling.

And I remember, this is a brand-new day.

Parenting Sources

Boosting Your Listening Power; Correspondent, July/August

Charting Your Family's Course. NACE, Costa Mesa, CA 714-546-5931

Getting Together, Building Relationships that Get to Yes; Fisher & Brown 1998

Health Wise Handbook and Systematic Stress Management; Burlington Northern R.R.

Holy Bible; God's Word written in various translations

How to Build Your Child's Self-Esteem; Dennis Waitley

How to Raise Happy Healthy Self-Confident Children; Brian Tracy, M.A. & Bettie B. Young, PhD.

How to Stop Being Teased and bullied without really trying, Israel C. Kalman, MS.

Light through an Eastern Window, Bishop Pilou

Overcoming Anger and Frustration; Dr. Paul Hauck

Parenting that Works, Edward R. Christophersen, PhD., and Susan L. Mortweet, PhD.,2003, American Psychological Association.

Parent Smart from the Heart Workshop & Parent Manual; Derek & Gail M.D. Randel

Playful Parenting, Lawrence J. Cohen, PhD.

Raising an Assertive Child - Facing the schoolyard bully: Samenow

Raising Children with Love and Limits; P. Catell, Ed.D.

The Five Love Languages; Gary Chapman

The Psychology of Achievement; Brian Tracy, M.A.

Twenty-One Ways to Diffuse Anger and Calm People Down; Career Track

Winning Without Intimidation; Bob Burg

Notes

Chapter 4 Spiritual Growth

These affirmations are designed to feed your spirit by applying God's word to your life, and, also improve your relationship with God and others.

Bonnie Bair, LCPC

God is with me. I like and accept myself. I am good. I am created in God's image and am forgiven through Christ Jesus.

I accept that feelings just are. By recognizing my feelings, I can deal with my emotions effectively. I realize hiding emotions can cause problems. Therefore, I recognize my feelings without blaming others. This allows me to take responsibility for my own attitudes and behavior.

I communicate my feelings desires and needs in a direct and honest manner, while considering the feelings of others.

I treat others and myself with respect. I value our differences and unique abilities and viewpoints. I seek win/win solutions and situations with others.

I allow others and myself to make mistakes, and learn from them. I confess my sins to God and others.

I am honest, direct, and considerate. I allow myself to ask God and others for help. I am confident to go before God's throne of Grace.

I stand up against evil, knowing it will flee from me. I repay wrongs with blessing, so I receive blessing.

When I want to be near God, I come near to God. I praise and worship God.

I am adorned with a gentle and quiet spirit. This is very precious to God.

Everything is clear and lies open before God. I do what is right and courageous.

I ask God for and receive mercy and grace. I seek God's face.

The days of my life are full of goodness and mercy.

I obey God and live in blessedness.

I am safe and secure. I am protected by divine love.

I create loving truthful communication.

As I nurture myself, others around me are nurtured. I relax into the flow of life and let God's love flow through me.

I lovingly care for my body, by eating foods that support my health.

I get plenty of rest and exercise.

I am patient, gentle, and kind.

I give to and serve others.

I speak well of myself and others.

I build my faith by hearing God's word, since faith comes from hearing God's word.

I count my blessings each day. I read the Bible and sing praises to God.

I am peaceable and have peace.

My heart is grounded in love.

I have a spirit of power, love, and a sound mind. I am strong on the inside.

I comprehend and know the love God has for me.

I understand God's word. I understand my blessings because of Christ Jesus.

I listen to others and respond in love, by acknowledging their feelings and needs.

I am humble and full of grace and mercy.

I serve others with a joyful heart.

I pray with and for others.

I know God's love and will for me.

I understand and trust God to give me exceedingly abundantly more than I ask or think.

I remember to think on things that are lovely and praiseworthy.

I remember all things work together for the good for those who are in Christ Jesus and that God is thinking about and watching everything that concerns me.

Spiritual Resources

Bi-Monthly Publication; Kate McVeigh Ministries

Holy Bible; God's word written in various translations

Inner Peace; Norman Vincent Peal

Chapter 5 Healing

These affirmations are designed to assist you in receiving the healing you seek. As you review them regularly, you will find your faith to grow and healing to come into your life.

Bonnie L. Bair, LCPC

I am created wonderfully by God, in his image, and am forgiven through Christ Jesus.

God's will, is for me to prosper and be in good health. Therefore, I prosper and am in good health.

God is with me. I am loved and safe.

I lovingly accept myself as I am, and others as they are.

I live in harmony with others.

I seek mutually satisfying relationships.

I appreciate others and their unique viewpoints.

I acknowledge and clearly express my own thoughts and feelings, with ease. Without blaming, I use "I statements," to express myself.

This allows me to handle emotions effectively, while being considerate of others.

I am quick to forgive and seek win/win solutions.

I am calm and satisfied.

I speak words of truth, am compassionate, and understanding.

I repay insult with blessing, so I receive blessing. I seek peace and pursue it.

I choose my thoughts and control my tongue, with ease.

I connect with God daily. I know God's love for me.

I do what I know to do. I pray about concerns and let go of them.

I make wise decisions and follow through.

I am good and do good works. I create loving communication.

I have a spirit of love, power and a sound mind.

I am patient with myself and others.

I ask for what I want and need, with love and ease.

I let go, forgive, and receive. I give and receive.

I stand tall and move in joy. I enjoy being me.

I take care of the things I need to do and trust God for time to do those things.

I willingly do the things I do with a cheerful heart. I smile and enjoy my day.

I understand that God is for me, protecting me, and is working miracles on my behalf.

I lovingly care for my body by eating foods that support my health and by getting proper rest and exercise.

I seek expertise and help, as needed, from others.

When I'm not feeling well, God's word encourages me to ask the leaders of the church to pray the prayer of faith and anoint me with oil.

I acknowledge sin to God and others. I ask for and receive forgiveness.

I know God's word. I partner with God to keep myself safe and do God's will. I allow myself to say "No" to others, at times. I take responsibility for my life – how I spend my time, what I watch, what I listen to, and say,

I resist temptation. I let go of fear and unbelief. I cling to what is good. I do what is right. I move into my greater good with ease. I enjoy God's plan for my life.

I ask God for what I desire and need, with thanksgiving and I receive it.

I am confident, capable and courageous. I enjoy learning and growing.

My body is beautiful, balanced and harmonious.

I breathe in divine inspiration and healing power.

Life flows through and around me, with ease. All things are possible.

I create peace in my mind, body, and our world.

My thoughts are pure. I concentrate on the things that are honorable, lovely, excellent, and praiseworthy.

I am tender, kind and affectionate.

I let go of tension through exercising, singing, dancing, playing, or laughing.

I relax my mind and body. I breathe in peace, joy, and love

I listen with love to my inner voice.

I am at peace with myself. Life is sweet.

God satisfies my desires with good things.

My youth is renewed like the eagles.

Healing Resources

Eleven Ways to Ease Your Nerves & Mind; National Assoc. for Mental Health

Health Wise Handbook & Systemic Stress Management; Burlington Northern RR

Holy Bible; God's word written in various translations

Inner Peace; Norman Vincent Peal

Overcoming Anger & Frustration; Dr. Paul Hauck

Stressed for Success; Penny Plautz

Stress Management & Relaxation Activities for Trainers; Epstein

You Can Heal Your Life; Louise Hay

Chapter 6   Relaxation

These affirmations are designed to help you relax and help bring healing to your body mind and relationships.

Bonnie L. Bair, LCPC

I allow my mind and body to relax.

I am a magnificent creation, created in God's image.

I am forgiven through Christ Jesus.

I accept myself and rejoice in who I am.

I ask God for all I need with thanksgiving and receive what I ask.

I enjoy life. I am good and I create good.

I relax and breathe in life, deeply and fully.

Love, joy, and peace are mine.

My life is balance and joyful.

There is time to do the things I want to do.

My thinking is centered and peaceful.

I write out ideas, and give anxieties to God.

I accept divine healing and peace.

I know and trust my needs and desires are being fulfilled.

I love life.

I enjoy being me and I enjoy new experiences.

Joy flows through my mind, body, and experience.

I speak with gentleness and love.

My body is healthy and balanced.

I exercise, sing, dance, play, and laugh.

My heart is young and my mind is sound.

I pray about every concern.

I am safe. God is for me. Everything happens at the right time.

I breathe in and out life, deeply and easily.

I lean back and put my left hand on my stomach and right hand on my chest. I breathe through my nose so that my left hand rises and I exhale through my mouth.

Since relaxation helps my body release tension and obtain greater balance; I say, "I am calm, clear, and centered." I slow down my breathing and breathe in healing energy. I receive peace.

I imagine myself in a beautiful peaceful place. I feel my muscles relax as pain and tension leaves my body.

I breathe in calm (soothing) energy, and my scalp and head relax.

I breathe in calm (soothing) energy, and my eyes and jaw relax.

I breathe in calm (soothing) energy, and my neck and shoulders relax.

I breathe in calm (soothing) energy, and my chest and arms relax.

I breathe in calm (soothing) energy, and my back and spine relax.

I breathe in calm (soothing) energy, and my wrists and hands relax.

I breathe in calm (soothing) energy, and my pelvis and hips relax.

I breathe in calm (soothing) energy, and my thighs and bottom relax.

I breathe in calm (soothing) energy, and my knees and ankles relax.

I breathe in calm (soothing) energy, and my feet, toes, and fingers relax.

I hold this relaxed feeling, by touching my thumb and index finger together.

I slip into peaceful sleep.

I sleep well and I awake refreshed and energized.

Relaxation Resources

Eleven Ways to Ease Your Nerves & Mind; National Assoc. for Mental Health

Health Wise Handbook & Systemic Stress Management; Burlington Northern RR

Holy Bible; God's word written in various translations

Inner Peace; Norman Vincent Peal

Overcoming Anger & Frustration; Dr. Paul Hauck

Stressed for Success; Penny Plautz

Stress Management & Relaxation Activities for Trainers; Epstein

You Can Heal Your Life; Louise Hay

Notes

www.ingramcontent.com/pod-product-compliance
Lightning Source LLC
LaVergne TN
LVHW051428080426
835508LV00022B/3294